Put That In Your Journal

· ·

A Women's Journey

Pamela Donelly

Bloomington, IN  Milton Keynes, UK

authorHOUSE®

AuthorHouse™
1663 Liberty Drive, Suite 200
Bloomington, IN 47403
www.authorhouse.com
Phone: 1-800-839-8640

AuthorHouse™ UK Ltd.
500 Avebury Boulevard
Central Milton Keynes, MK9 2BE
www.authorhouse.co.uk
Phone: 08001974150

First published by AuthorHouse 3/13/2007

ISBN: 978-1-4259-9457-0 (sc)
ISBN: 978-1-4259-9456-3 (hc)

Printed in the United States of America
Bloomington, Indiana

This book is printed on acid-free paper.

....

I once read a book called the Ex Wifes Survival Guide by Debby Holt. I bought this book just because I loved the title being an ex wife. I found in this book to have humor in the aftermath of divorce. Divorce is a journey with a magnitude of emotions including anger, hurt, remorse, sadness, etc., even if it was your decision to split. Lets face it, it is a life altering decision. I also love Nora Ephron's good humor and wit. She says " Never marry a man you wouldn't want to be divorced from." and "The minute you decide to get divorced go see a lawyer and file the papers." She says the things most people think about but never say. I admire that in a person. She also says " Write everything down." and " Keep a journal." That is exactly what we are doing.

I found out several things during my journey of divorce, actually a lot of things but this is not a self help book and we would be here for days if I told you my whole story. I just found it was extremely important to keep a journal during and even after my divorce, I have even encouraged my kids to do the same. I have felt more content with my life by keeping a journal. The first thing to remember is to take time for yourself. I know how hard it is especially if you have kids or work outside of the home. It was life saving for me when I was drowning in self pity, loneliness, paying bills, and struggling with kids, being the full time cook, maid, chauffeur, and therapist. You see their father wasn't as involved in their lives as much as they would have liked. They also didn't see him that much, so I did not get a lot of alone time, but I did make time for certain things.

My lifeline has been my girlfriends. I have had a great support group of friends. We get together about every two to three weeks usually for dinner. We all have our war stories, we share, laugh, and cry. It is amazing what a night out with the girls can do. Usually better than most dates I have been on. I have found through divorce I have lost a lot of people in my life but in return I have found true friends that I know I can count on.

I found a therapist who I just love. She is a wonderful woman that I truly admire. She has been tough on me when I have needed it, but has also made me see things about who I am and what I can be. She has gotten me through some extremely tough times. She has helped me gain the confidence to try new things, be brave, and move on. She also taught me that it is ok to make time for myself. Janet-thank you!!!

Activities are great also, whether it is ceramics, a class at your local college, a book club, or a church group. Find something you enjoy doing, it is also a great way to meet people. My outlet is exercise. I never knew I loved it so much. Walking, running, kickboxing, weights. I love it all! It has helped me to get back in shape, body and mind. It also is a quick fix for all that frustration, especially when you are punching! And it is so good for you at the same time.

And of course my children who I love more than anything. They are the light of my life and I thank God for them everyday. Their love and support has gotten me through the last few years.

When I was going through my divorce it helped to keep a journal of everyday events, and believe me it came in handy. One of my closest friends is an attorney. Everyday she would check on me and encourage me to write anything down that had anything to do with my divorce. I did at first to humor her. I then realized it made me feel better getting it on paper when it was fresh. I would also write why whatever happened made me angry, and how it hurt me. When I started writing I was very disorganized. I realized from my mistakes I needed more of a format, learning to note the date and the time.Then my oldest and dearest friend (I mean oldest as in how long we have known each other, over 30 years) started going through her seperation. I started encouraging her to write everything down. She then inspired me to write this, and I thank her for that. You need to keep track of expenses also. I found as my children got older (I have three) their needs became more expensive which I had not considered when we formed a budget during our divorce agreement. I never considered cell phones, computers, vacations, allowances, gas and wear and tear on my car driving my children where they needed to go, entertaining their friends, their animals, sports, and activities. My son loves anything electronic, and we all know that stuff is not cheap. Having two daughters, one a teenager, and one not far behind, their needs became increasingly more expensive. Their clothes, (and they love to shop as most girls do), their toiletries, make up, hair, and nails are now an essential part of their daily routine. I should have considered these things being a woman myself. Ha! Ha! Just a few things to keep in mind.

I have put funny expressions at the bottom of the pages, some you may have heard before and some my friends and I came up with. I hope they make you smile. Divorce is never fun, but sometimes if you can put a funny spin on a bad situation even for a minute it makes life a little easier. Each day does get a little better.

Use this book to organize your thoughts. Use it to keep track of the date, time, expenses, and even mileage on your car. I hope it helps you as it helped me.

When in doubt buy shoes.

Life takes many turns, you just have to accept them and try and keep a positive outlook.

The future belongs to those who believe
in the beauty of their dreams.

Life is short – Eat dessert first.

Crazy doesn't begin to cover it.

I know right from and wrong, and
wrong is usually the fun one.

Ever notice how " What the hell is
always the right answer."

Isn't it funny how women with kids going through a divorce are usually the ones to put their life on hold.

Just think you get half the money and you
don't have to live with him anymore.

Shhhh — A great secret — there is no downside to divorce.

Married women and men would get along better if we lived in separate houses.

A good marriage fits all, a bad one
comes in many criticizes.

The only reason men and women get
together is because the parts fit.

What goes around comes around — we can only hope.

Things happen, we don't get do overs, you can't turn back time. The only thing you can change is how you let them affect you.

People in glass houses shouldn't throw stones.

No matter how much weight you gain or
loose shoes and purses always fit.

With true friends even water shared has a sweet taste.

While you are waiting for the right guy — have fun with the wrong ones in the meantime.

Good girls go to heaven, bad girls go everywhere.

The only thing better than a martini is two martinis.

Don't sweat the small stuff.

Of course you are my best friend – you know to much!

Men, chocolate, and coffee — the richer the better.

Many of life's failures are people who did not realize
how close they were to success when they gave up.

Nothing better than a piece of Godiva
to get you through the day.

Champagne and strawberries — a match made in heaven.

Don't worry his day will come, all dogs don't go to heaven.

Whatever did we do before $5.00 cups of coffee?

Diamonds are a girls best friend, set in platinum of course.

Men come and go, jewelry is forever.

An expensive bottle of champagne is great, finding one you like for under $20.00 is even better.

Two may talk together under the same roof for many years yet never really meet, and two others at first speech are old friends.

God gave us our relatives, thank God
we can choose our friends.

Is white chocolate really chocolate?

What is the point of decaf?

Stay in the right hand lane unless you are going at least ten miles over the speed limit.

Having a relationship with some men
is like having a second job.

Why do men love bitches?

Love is not a Hallmark card, it is a battlefield.

....

Even the good men are not that great.

I don't agree with it, but I understand why women are gay.

Women need a reason for sex, men just need a place.

The question where is this going? Is relationship suicide.

It is better to be disliked for who you are,
then to be loved for who you are not.

It is always fun to shop with a buddy, she
can help justify what you spend.

Helping one another is a part of the
religion of the sisterhood.

When people are ready to, they change.
They never do it before.

Let's face it, a man is always going to be a better man for the next one, but they need to stop rubbing our noses in it.

....

I have been searching outward, not
inward and I am so tired.

Never go shopping without room on your credit card.

···

When women are depressed, they eat or go
shopping. Men drink and get other women pregnant.
It is a whole different way of thinking.

Men and women are really two cultures and their way of thinking are completely different.

....

Shopping isn't only good for buying things, it is good for socializing and boosting the economy.

Marrying a man is like buying something you've been admiring for a long time in a shop window. You may love it when you get it home, but it doesn't always go with everything in the house.

" Because I am the mother that's why!

A good friend will always tell you when
you have spinach in your teeth.

It's called a break up because it's broken.

It's not the years of your life that
counts it's the life in your years.

PMS — Peculiar Mental State

Free yourself from habits that supress you people
that depress you and rules that repress you.

The rules are that there are no rules to dating,
something I had to learn all over again.

Free yourself from relationships that drain,
people that take and never give.

Get rid of clothes that pinch!

Don't explain, don't justify, just take a nap.

If you obey all the rules you will miss all the fun.

Lead me not into temptation. I can find it myself.

I love a martini, but two at the most. Three, I'm under the table, four, I'm under the host.

If you are not happy in yourself, the latest Jimmy Choo or Prada creation won't change anything.

The end-all be-all for most women is to be in a loving relationship with someone who is your equal and will help carry the load.

Some nights I would rather sit home and take my chance of not meeting Mr. Right than meeting ten Mr. Wrongs.

You oviously have me confused with someone who cares.

Live, Laugh, Love!

There are lots of good men — ok, good enough.

Ben & Jerry — now those are men
worthy of a women's trust.

The difference between men and shoes is
that you can fall out of love with men.

Menopause, menstruate, menial, mental, notice
what these words all have in common.

Ever notice skin care labels for women over 40? They say wrinkles that arrive with age. Like we invite them and throw a party.

You can order more then one dessert!

Some days I am a woman on the edge. Some days I
am mother of the year. Usually not the same days.

The empty nest is underrated.

Flings are like firecrackers — once flung you
usually don't get a second bang of it.

Anything you think is wrong with your body
at 30 you will wish you had at 40.

You know you have a best friend when
you can call her at 2:00 a.m.

If the shoe doesn't fit in the store
it isn't going to fit at home.

When our girlfriends call for help we rush to
the rescue. Sister down, sisters rally.

I think I am misunderstood or everyone
else just doesn't speak bitch.

I am so sick of every man on the face of the earth and if I could kick everyone of them in the crotch and watch them keel over in pain I would shriek with delight. Did I mention I am bitter?

A midlife crisis checklist — Get a divorce,
discover a lifetime of humor, start a new life
plan, Spend more time with girlfriends, have a
mind blowing affair, and enjoy yourself!

Just say "So what."

Move on. Don't spend time on situations
you can't change. Enough said.

Each day give yourself time to laugh.

Keep a pen and paper handy. Those who keep a journal feel more in control, and are missing less.

Spending your time in the past imagining what could have been leaves you unhappy. Think instead of how to improve your future.

It's not what you wear it's how you accessorize.

Fairy tales can come true, in life we need to trust
in ourselves, embrace our faults, and brazen it
out with courage, strength, bravery and truth.

Accentuate, don't exaggerate.

Keep your friends close and your enemies closer.

Amazing how spending some money, especially
when you haven't got it can perk you right up.

Real men don't need to boast about
their qualities, it is apparent.

It is pathetic when a man's ego is so bruised he has to lie about the woman who has had enough to make himself feel better.

Love is like a scary ride — when you are on you want to get off, and when you are off you want to get back on.

Any woman can look her best if she feels good in her skin. It's not a question of clothes or make up. It's how she sparkles.

So long as a woman has twinkles in her eyes, no man notices whether she has wrinkles under them.

We all have moments of desperation. But if we can face them head on, that's when we find out how strong we really are.

Taking the high road sometimes is overrated,
I say let the bitch have it.

Being married and unable to shop is probably
the worst of all possible worlds.

Become the most positive and
enthusiastic person you know.

Drink champagne for no reason at all.

Don't be afraid to say " I made a mistake."

Real men will travel to you.

Good friends support each other after they have been humiliated. Great friends pretend nothing happened.

I tried poor but happy. Guess what? Not that happy.

Make new friends but cherish the old ones.

Think big thoughts but relish small pleasures.

Live your life as an exclamation not an explanation.

Stop blaming others, take responsibility
for every area of your life.

Everyone has a little dirty laundry.

Isn't there a rule that some people don't actually have to be married or in love? There has to be a few that actually manage to live happily ever after all by themselves. Don't they? Someone, somewhere must!

I am not bitter, I am mad as hell!

It isn't funny if I'm not laughing!

When a man buys a woman expensive jewelry there are many things he wants in return. Conversation isn't one of them.

Who cares what people think. It is only the opinion of the ones you care about that matters, everyone else can go to hell.

A nice round butt, now there is a
real symbol of womanhood.

Mirror, mirror on the wall, I am my mother after all.

You can't make sane out of crazy.

Mothering — Some days I am just not
wired for this and I want to quit.

Be comfortable with yourself!

Dreams are how we figure out where we want to go.
Life is how we get there. Allow time for traffic.

You can't amaze the world unless
you first surprise yourself.

A little bit of money, a pinch of ass
kissing, stir — instant respect.

Remember in a divorce that $20.00 garden hose you are fighting over will end up costing you $ 20,000.00 in attorney fees.

Dear Santa, – Manolos, – Jimmy Choos, –
Chanel bag, Oh!...............and world peace.

A divorce involving children — No wonder
some species eat their young.

A child that says they can play an instrument
with their eyes closed, probably is.

Hug your kids everyday even if they don't hug back.

....

Have a family dinner together once a week,
no t.v. or phone, and sit down!

Be a bobble head and "you're right" them to death, they can't argue back and it will drive them nuts. This works on kids and ex husbands.

....
Keep lots of Aspirin, Motrin, Midol and Tylenol P.M. handy.

Ever notice you are full until the dessert menu arrives.

Have a girls night as often as you can,
champagne, food and a box of tissues.

I am finding with age and wisdom for the sake of your kids, sometimes you just need to suck it up and get along with your ex.

Life is what you make it — for a long time I saw the glass as half empty, now I see it half full and want it to overflow so I can suck the foam off.

"WHATEVER WORKS!"

First of all, I am not 100% in love with your tone right now.

Bitter with Baggage seeks same. My
daughter asked what this meant. I said Bitter
would be me, baggage would be you.

Your inner bitch is the little black dress of
attitudes, perfect for any occasion.

You know why shopping is better than sex? If you are not satisfied for any reason you can return it for something you like better.

Mid life crisis for a man is just one
more excuse to tick us off.

When challenged, react calmly and get them later.

Mid life brings wisdom to know that life throws us curves and we are sitting on our biggest ones.

....

A man with money is great, as long as he is great.
Remember you can't sleep with your jewelry.

Mid life is when you look at your mouthy,
eyeball rolling, text messaging teenager and
think — I have stretch marks for this!

Men are like a fine wine. They begin as grapes, and it's up to women to stomp the shit out of them until they turn into something acceptable to have dinner with.

Laugh and the world laughs with you,
cry and your mascara runs.

Top 5 Reasons Women Drink – cheating men, lying men, insensitive men, helpless men, lack of men. See a pattern?

Be naughty, save Santa the trip!

It would be nice to hear from a man
— No secrets, just surprises!

Three things you want out of life — A man that turns you on, a man that you trust, and a man that makes you laugh, and hope that the three will never meet.

....

And ladies, finally, live life to its fullest, don't settle, be true to yourself, and don't be your own worst enemy where men are concerned.

www.ingramcontent.com/pod-product-compliance
Lightning Source LLC
Chambersburg PA
CBHW061250280526
45784CB00002B/711